Sometimes life gets busy, and we lose focus. We forget God's faithfulness, or we struggle to hold God's truth within our hearts. The goal of this journal is to help you discover God's truth and engrave His promises on your heart and mind. My hope is that you will not only know God's word, but may you also grow closer to the God who knows you and apply God's truth to your life.

You will notice that there are only 5 days for each week to give grace for a missed day or a busy schedule. Each day will have five sections of work to do with your reading.

- **Read:** I will give you a specific section/chapter of God's Word to read.
- **Scripture:** What is one verse that stood out to you today?
- **Truth:** What is one truth that you discovered about God or about life from today's reading?
- **Trust:** What is one thing that you need to trust God with today?
- **Praise:** What is one thing that you can praise God for today?

Week 1: Day One

Read: Proverbs 1; Psalm 8

Scripture: What is one verse that stood out to you today?

Truth: What is one truth that you discovered about God or about life from today's reading?

Trust: What is one thing that you need to trust God with today?

Praise: What is one thing that you can praise God for today?

Week 1: Day Two

Read: Genesis 1-2

Scripture: What is one verse that stood out to you today?

Truth: What is one truth that you discovered about God or about life from today's reading?

Trust: What is one thing that you need to trust God with today?

Praise: What is one thing that you can praise God for today?

Week 1: Day Three

Read: John 1

Scripture: What is one verse that stood out to you today?

Truth: What is one truth that you discovered about God or about life from today's reading?

Trust: What is one thing that you need to trust God with today?

Praise: What is one thing that you can praise God for today?

Week 1: Day Four

Read: Romans 1-2

Scripture: What is one verse that stood out to you today?

Truth: What is one truth that you discovered about God or about life from today's reading?

Trust: What is one thing that you need to trust God with today?

Praise: What is one thing that you can praise God for today?

Week 1: Day Five

Read: Isaiah 1, Isaiah 8:11-9:7

Scripture: What is one verse that stood out to you today?

Truth: What is one truth that you discovered about God or about life from today's reading?

Trust: What is one thing that you need to trust God with today?

Praise: What is one thing that you can praise God for today?

Week 1 Review

Memorization: What is one or two verses that you want to memorize or write on your mind?

Application: How have you applied God's truth to your life this past week?

Praise: How has God helped or answered prayers this week?

Week 2: Day One

Read: Proverbs 2; Psalm 18

Scripture: What is one verse that stood out to you today?

Truth: What is one truth that you discovered about God or about life from today's reading?

Trust: What is one thing that you need to trust God with today?

Praise: What is one thing that you can praise God for today?

Week 2: Day Two

Read: Genesis 3-4

Scripture: What is one verse that stood out to you today?

Truth: What is one truth that you discovered about God or about life from today's reading?

Trust: What is one thing that you need to trust God with today?

Praise: What is one thing that you can praise God for today?

Week 2: Day Three

Read: John 3-4

Scripture: What is one verse that stood out to you today?

Truth: What is one truth that you discovered about God or about life from today's reading?

Trust: What is one thing that you need to trust God with today?

Praise: What is one thing that you can praise God for today?

Week 2: Day Four

Read: Romans 3-5

Scripture: What is one verse that stood out to you today?

Truth: What is one truth that you discovered about God or about life from today's reading?

Trust: What is one thing that you need to trust God with today?

Praise: What is one thing that you can praise God for today?

Week 2: Day Five

Read: 1 Thessalonians 4-5; 2 Thessalonians 3

Scripture: What is one verse that stood out to you today?

Truth: What is one truth that you discovered about God or about life from today's reading?

Trust: What is one thing that you need to trust God with today?

Praise: What is one thing that you can praise God for today?

Week 2 Review

Memorization: What is one or two verses that you want to memorize or write on your mind?

Application: How have you applied God's truth to your life this past week?

Praise: How has God helped or answered prayers this week?

Week 3: Day One

Read: Proverbs 3; Psalm 19; Psalm 25

Scripture: What is one verse that stood out to you today?

Truth: What is one truth that you discovered about God or about life from today's reading?

Trust: What is one thing that you need to trust God with today?

Praise: What is one thing that you can praise God for today?

Week 3: Day Two

Read: Genesis 6:9-9:17

Scripture: What is one verse that stood out to you today?

Truth: What is one truth that you discovered about God or about life from today's reading?

Trust: What is one thing that you need to trust God with today?

Praise: What is one thing that you can praise God for today?

Week 3: Day Three

Read: John 5-7

Scripture: What is one verse that stood out to you today?

Truth: What is one truth that you discovered about God or about life from today's reading?

Trust: What is one thing that you need to trust God with today?

Praise: What is one thing that you can praise God for today?

Week 3: Day Four

Read: Romans 6-7

Scripture: What is one verse that stood out to you today?

Truth: What is one truth that you discovered about God or about life from today's reading?

Trust: What is one thing that you need to trust God with today?

Praise: What is one thing that you can praise God for today?

Week 3: Day Five

Read: Isaiah 25:1-26:19

Scripture: What is one verse that stood out to you today?

Truth: What is one truth that you discovered about God or about life from today's reading?

Trust: What is one thing that you need to trust God with today?

Praise: What is one thing that you can praise God for today?

Week 3 Review

Memorization: What is one or two verses that you want to memorize or write on your mind?

Application: How have you applied God's truth to your life this past week?

Praise: How has God helped or answered prayers this week?

Week 4: Day One

Read: Proverbs 4; Psalm 27

Scripture: What is one verse that stood out to you today?

Truth: What is one truth that you discovered about God or about life from today's reading?

Trust: What is one thing that you need to trust God with today?

Praise: What is one thing that you can praise God for today?

Week 4: Day Two

Read: Genesis 17 and 21-22

Scripture: What is one verse that stood out to you today?

Truth: What is one truth that you discovered about God or about life from today's reading?

Trust: What is one thing that you need to trust God with today?

Praise: What is one thing that you can praise God for today?

Week 4: Day Three

Read: John 9-10

Scripture: What is one verse that stood out to you today?

Truth: What is one truth that you discovered about God or about life from today's reading?

Trust: What is one thing that you need to trust God with today?

Praise: What is one thing that you can praise God for today?

Week 4: Day Four

Read: Romans 8

Scripture: What is one verse that stood out to you today?

Truth: What is one truth that you discovered about God or about life from today's reading?

Trust: What is one thing that you need to trust God with today?

Praise: What is one thing that you can praise God for today?

Week 4: Day Five

Read: 1 Timothy 1, 2, and 4

Scripture: What is one verse that stood out to you today?

Truth: What is one truth that you discovered about God or about life from today's reading?

Trust: What is one thing that you need to trust God with today?

Praise: What is one thing that you can praise God for today?

Week 4 Review

Memorization: What is one or two verses that you want to
memorize or write on your mind?

Application: How have you applied God's truth to your life
this past week?

Praise: How has God helped or answered prayers this week?

Week 5: Day One

Read: Proverbs 5; Psalm 27-28

Scripture: What is one verse that stood out to you today?

Truth: What is one truth that you discovered about God or about life from today's reading?

Trust: What is one thing that you need to trust God with today?

Praise: What is one thing that you can praise God for today?

Week 5: Day Two

Read: Genesis 37, 39

Scripture: What is one verse that stood out to you today?

Truth: What is one truth that you discovered about God or about life from today's reading?

Trust: What is one thing that you need to trust God with today?

Praise: What is one thing that you can praise God for today?

Week 5: Day Three

Read: Matthew 5-6

Scripture: What is one verse that stood out to you today?

Truth: What is one truth that you discovered about God or about life from today's reading?

Trust: What is one thing that you need to trust God with today?

Praise: What is one thing that you can praise God for today?

Week 5: Day Four

Read: Romans 12

Scripture: What is one verse that stood out to you today?

Truth: What is one truth that you discovered about God or about life from today's reading?

Trust: What is one thing that you need to trust God with today?

Praise: What is one thing that you can praise God for today?

Week 5: Day Five

Read: 2 Timothy 1-2

Scripture: What is one verse that stood out to you today?

Truth: What is one truth that you discovered about God or about life from today's reading?

Trust: What is one thing that you need to trust God with today?

Praise: What is one thing that you can praise God for today?

Week 5 Review

Memorization: What is one or two verses that you want to memorize or write on your mind?

Application: How have you applied God's truth to your life this past week?

Praise: How has God helped or answered prayers this week?

Week 6: Day One

Read: Proverbs 6; Psalm 36

Scripture: What is one verse that stood out to you today?

Truth: What is one truth that you discovered about God or about life from today's reading?

Trust: What is one thing that you need to trust God with today?

Praise: What is one thing that you can praise God for today?

Week 6: Day Two

Read: Genesis 41:37-42:38

Scripture: What is one verse that stood out to you today?

Truth: What is one truth that you discovered about God or about life from today's reading?

Trust: What is one thing that you need to trust God with today?

Praise: What is one thing that you can praise God for today?

Week 6: Day Three

Read: Matthew 7

Scripture: What is one verse that stood out to you today?

Truth: What is one truth that you discovered about God or about life from today's reading?

Trust: What is one thing that you need to trust God with today?

Praise: What is one thing that you can praise God for today?

Week 6: Day Four

Read: Romans 13-14

Scripture: What is one verse that stood out to you today?

Truth: What is one truth that you discovered about God or about life from today's reading?

Trust: What is one thing that you need to trust God with today?

Praise: What is one thing that you can praise God for today?

Week 6: Day Five

Read: 2 Timothy 3-4

Scripture: What is one verse that stood out to you today?

Truth: What is one truth that you discovered about God or about life from today's reading?

Trust: What is one thing that you need to trust God with today?

Praise: What is one thing that you can praise God for today?

Week 6 Review

Memorization: What is one or two verses that you want to memorize or write on your mind?

Application: How have you applied God's truth to your life this past week?

Praise: How has God helped or answered prayers this week?

Week 7: Day One

Read: Proverbs 7; Psalm 40

Scripture: What is one verse that stood out to you today?

Truth: What is one truth that you discovered about God or about life from today's reading?

Trust: What is one thing that you need to trust God with today?

Praise: What is one thing that you can praise God for today?

Week 7: Day Two

Read: Genesis 43:1-45:15

Scripture: What is one verse that stood out to you today?

Truth: What is one truth that you discovered about God or about life from today's reading?

Trust: What is one thing that you need to trust God with today?

Praise: What is one thing that you can praise God for today?

Week 7: Day Three

Read: Matthew 8-10

Scripture: What is one verse that stood out to you today?

Truth: What is one truth that you discovered about God or about life from today's reading?

Trust: What is one thing that you need to trust God with today?

Praise: What is one thing that you can praise God for today?

Week 7: Day Four

Read: Romans 15-16

Scripture: What is one verse that stood out to you today?

Truth: What is one truth that you discovered about God or about life from today's reading?

Trust: What is one thing that you need to trust God with today?

Praise: What is one thing that you can praise God for today?

Week 7: Day Five

Read: Isaiah 40-41

Scripture: What is one verse that stood out to you today?

Truth: What is one truth that you discovered about God or about life from today's reading?

Trust: What is one thing that you need to trust God with today?

Praise: What is one thing that you can praise God for today?

Week 7 Review

Memorization: What is one or two verses that you want to
memorize or write on your mind?

Application: How have you applied God's truth to your life
this past week?

Praise: How has God helped or answered prayers this week?

Week 8: Day One

Read: Proverbs 8; Psalm 42-43

Scripture: What is one verse that stood out to you today?

Truth: What is one truth that you discovered about God or about life from today's reading?

Trust: What is one thing that you need to trust God with today?

Praise: What is one thing that you can praise God for today?

Week 8: Day Two

Read: Exodus 1-2

Scripture: What is one verse that stood out to you today?

Truth: What is one truth that you discovered about God or about life from today's reading?

Trust: What is one thing that you need to trust God with today?

Praise: What is one thing that you can praise God for today?

Week 8: Day Three

Read: Matthew 11-12

Scripture: What is one verse that stood out to you today?

Truth: What is one truth that you discovered about God or about life from today's reading?

Trust: What is one thing that you need to trust God with today?

Praise: What is one thing that you can praise God for today?

Week 8: Day Four

Read: 1 Corinthians 1-2

Scripture: What is one verse that stood out to you today?

Truth: What is one truth that you discovered about God or about life from today's reading?

Trust: What is one thing that you need to trust God with today?

Praise: What is one thing that you can praise God for today?

Week 8: Day Five

Read: 1 John 1-2

Scripture: What is one verse that stood out to you today?

Truth: What is one truth that you discovered about God or about life from today's reading?

Trust: What is one thing that you need to trust God with today?

Praise: What is one thing that you can praise God for today?

Week 8 Review

Memorization: What is one or two verses that you want to memorize or write on your mind?

Application: How have you applied God's truth to your life this past week?

Praise: How has God helped or answered prayers this week?

Week 9: Day One

Read: Proverbs 9; Psalm 46

Scripture: What is one verse that stood out to you today?

Truth: What is one truth that you discovered about God or about life from today's reading?

Trust: What is one thing that you need to trust God with today?

Praise: What is one thing that you can praise God for today?

Week 9: Day Two

Read: Exodus 3-4

Scripture: What is one verse that stood out to you today?

Truth: What is one truth that you discovered about God or about life from today's reading?

Trust: What is one thing that you need to trust God with today?

Praise: What is one thing that you can praise God for today?

Week 9: Day Three

Read: Matthew 13

Scripture: What is one verse that stood out to you today?

Truth: What is one truth that you discovered about God or about life from today's reading?

Trust: What is one thing that you need to trust God with today?

Praise: What is one thing that you can praise God for today?

Week 9: Day Four

Read: 1 Corinthians 10-11

Scripture: What is one verse that stood out to you today?

Truth: What is one truth that you discovered about God or about life from today's reading?

Trust: What is one thing that you need to trust God with today?

Praise: What is one thing that you can praise God for today?

Week 9: Day Five

Read: Isaiah 42-43

Scripture: What is one verse that stood out to you today?

Truth: What is one truth that you discovered about God or about life from today's reading?

Trust: What is one thing that you need to trust God with today?

Praise: What is one thing that you can praise God for today?

Week 9 Review

Memorization: What is one or two verses that you want to memorize or write on your mind?

Application: How have you applied God's truth to your life this past week?

Praise: How has God helped or answered prayers this week?

Week 10 Stop and Reflect

Scripture: What verses have helped you the last two months?

Truth: What truths from God's Word have you seen appear in real life in the last two months?

Praise: How have you seen God work in your life in the last two months?

Requests: What is your prayer for this week?
What do you want to ask God to do?

Week 11: Day One

Read: Proverbs 10:1-13; Psalm 51, 63

Scripture: What is one verse that stood out to you today?

Truth: What is one truth that you discovered about God or about life from today's reading?

Trust: What is one thing that you need to trust God with today?

Praise: What is one thing that you can praise God for today?

Week 11: Day Two

Read: Exodus 14-15

Scripture: What is one verse that stood out to you today?

Truth: What is one truth that you discovered about God or about life from today's reading?

Trust: What is one thing that you need to trust God with today?

Praise: What is one thing that you can praise God for today?

Week 11: Day Three

Read: Matthew 14:13-15:20

Scripture: What is one verse that stood out to you today?

Truth: What is one truth that you discovered about God or about life from today's reading?

Trust: What is one thing that you need to trust God with today?

Praise: What is one thing that you can praise God for today?

Week 11: Day Four

Read: 1 Corinthians 12-14

Scripture: What is one verse that stood out to you today?

Truth: What is one truth that you discovered about God or about life from today's reading?

Trust: What is one thing that you need to trust God with today?

Praise: What is one thing that you can praise God for today?

Week 11: Day Five

Read: 1 John 3-4

Scripture: What is one verse that stood out to you today?

Truth: What is one truth that you discovered about God or about life from today's reading?

Trust: What is one thing that you need to trust God with today?

Praise: What is one thing that you can praise God for today?

Week 11 Review

Memorization: What is one or two verses that you want to memorize or write on your mind?

Application: How have you applied God's truth to your life this past week?

Praise: How has God helped or answered prayers this week?

Week 12: Day One

Read: Proverbs 10:14-32; Psalm 65 and 82

Scripture: What is one verse that stood out to you today?

Truth: What is one truth that you discovered about God or about life from today's reading?

Trust: What is one thing that you need to trust God with today?

Praise: What is one thing that you can praise God for today?

Week 12: Day Two

Read: Exodus 19:1-20:21

Scripture: What is one verse that stood out to you today?

Truth: What is one truth that you discovered about God or about life from today's reading?

Trust: What is one thing that you need to trust God with today?

Praise: What is one thing that you can praise God for today?

Week 12: Day Three

Read: Matthew 18-19

Scripture: What is one verse that stood out to you today?

Truth: What is one truth that you discovered about God or about life from today's reading?

Trust: What is one thing that you need to trust God with today?

Praise: What is one thing that you can praise God for today?

Week 12: Day Four

Read: 2 Corinthians 4

Scripture: What is one verse that stood out to you today?

Truth: What is one truth that you discovered about God or about life from today's reading?

Trust: What is one thing that you need to trust God with today?

Praise: What is one thing that you can praise God for today?

Week 12: Day Five

Read: Isaiah 44-46

Scripture: What is one verse that stood out to you today?

Truth: What is one truth that you discovered about God or about life from today's reading?

Trust: What is one thing that you need to trust God with today?

Praise: What is one thing that you can praise God for today?

Week 12 Review

Memorization: What is one or two verses that you want to memorize or write on your mind?

Application: How have you applied God's truth to your life this past week?

Praise: How has God helped or answered prayers this week?

Week 13: Day One

Read: Proverbs 11:1-21; Psalm 84-85

Scripture: What is one verse that stood out to you today?

Truth: What is one truth that you discovered about God or about life from today's reading?

Trust: What is one thing that you need to trust God with today?

Praise: What is one thing that you can praise God for today?

Week 13: Day Two

Read: Exodus 32-33

Scripture: What is one verse that stood out to you today?

Truth: What is one truth that you discovered about God or about life from today's reading?

Trust: What is one thing that you need to trust God with today?

Praise: What is one thing that you can praise God for today?

Week 13: Day Three

Read: Matthew 20

Scripture: What is one verse that stood out to you today?

Truth: What is one truth that you discovered about God or about life from today's reading?

Trust: What is one thing that you need to trust God with today?

Praise: What is one thing that you can praise God for today?

Week 13: Day Four

Read: 2 Corinthians 5-6

Scripture: What is one verse that stood out to you today?

Truth: What is one truth that you discovered about God or about life from today's reading?

Trust: What is one thing that you need to trust God with today?

Praise: What is one thing that you can praise God for today?

Week 13: Day Five

Read: 1 John 5

Scripture: What is one verse that stood out to you today?

Truth: What is one truth that you discovered about God or about life from today's reading?

Trust: What is one thing that you need to trust God with today?

Praise: What is one thing that you can praise God for today?

Week 13 Review

Memorization: What is one or two verses that you want to memorize or write on your mind?

Application: How have you applied God's truth to your life this past week?

Praise: How has God helped or answered prayers this week?

Week 14: Day One

Read: Proverbs 11:22-31; Psalm 86

Scripture: What is one verse that stood out to you today?

Truth: What is one truth that you discovered about God or about life from today's reading?

Trust: What is one thing that you need to trust God with today?

Praise: What is one thing that you can praise God for today?

Week 14: Day Two

Read: Joshua 1-2

Scripture: What is one verse that stood out to you today?

Truth: What is one truth that you discovered about God or about life from today's reading?

Trust: What is one thing that you need to trust God with today?

Praise: What is one thing that you can praise God for today?

Week 14: Day Three

Read: Matthew 21

Scripture: What is one verse that stood out to you today?

Truth: What is one truth that you discovered about God or about life from today's reading?

Trust: What is one thing that you need to trust God with today?

Praise: What is one thing that you can praise God for today?

Week 14: Day Four

Read: 2 Corinthians 12-13

Scripture: What is one verse that stood out to you today?

Truth: What is one truth that you discovered about God or about life from today's reading?

Trust: What is one thing that you need to trust God with today?

Praise: What is one thing that you can praise God for today?

Week 14: Day Five

Read: Isaiah 48-49

Scripture: What is one verse that stood out to you today?

Truth: What is one truth that you discovered about God or about life from today's reading?

Trust: What is one thing that you need to trust God with today?

Praise: What is one thing that you can praise God for today?

Week 14 Review

Memorization: What is one or two verses that you want to memorize or write on your mind?

Application: How have you applied God's truth to your life this past week?

Praise: How has God helped or answered prayers this week?

Week 15: Day One

Read: Proverbs 12:1-16; Psalm 91-92

Scripture: What is one verse that stood out to you today?

Truth: What is one truth that you discovered about God or about life from today's reading?

Trust: What is one thing that you need to trust God with today?

Praise: What is one thing that you can praise God for today?

Week 15: Day Two

Read: Joshua 6

Scripture: What is one verse that stood out to you today?

Truth: What is one truth that you discovered about God or about life from today's reading?

Trust: What is one thing that you need to trust God with today?

Praise: What is one thing that you can praise God for today?

Week 15: Day Three

Read: Matthew 22-23

Scripture: What is one verse that stood out to you today?

Truth: What is one truth that you discovered about God or about life from today's reading?

Trust: What is one thing that you need to trust God with today?

Praise: What is one thing that you can praise God for today?

Week 15: Day Four

Read: Galatians 1:6-16; 2:15-21

Scripture: What is one verse that stood out to you today?

Truth: What is one truth that you discovered about God or about life from today's reading?

Trust: What is one thing that you need to trust God with today?

Praise: What is one thing that you can praise God for today?

Week 15: Day Five

Read: Isaiah 51-52

Scripture: What is one verse that stood out to you today?

Truth: What is one truth that you discovered about God or about life from today's reading?

Trust: What is one thing that you need to trust God with today?

Praise: What is one thing that you can praise God for today?

Week 15 Review

Memorization: What is one or two verses that you want to memorize or write on your mind?

Application: How have you applied God's truth to your life this past week?

Praise: How has God helped or answered prayers this week?

Week 1: Day One

Read: Proverbs 1; Psalm 8

Scripture: What is one verse that stood out to you today?

Truth: What is one truth that you discovered about God or about life from today's reading?

Trust: What is one thing that you need to trust God with today?

Praise: What is one thing that you can praise God for today?

Week 1: Day Two

Read: Genesis 1-2

Scripture: What is one verse that stood out to you today?

Truth: What is one truth that you discovered about God or about life from today's reading?

Trust: What is one thing that you need to trust God with today?

Praise: What is one thing that you can praise God for today?

Week 1: Day Three

Read: John 1

Scripture: What is one verse that stood out to you today?

Truth: What is one truth that you discovered about God or about life from today's reading?

Trust: What is one thing that you need to trust God with today?

Praise: What is one thing that you can praise God for today?

Week 1: Day Four

Read: Romans 1-2

Scripture: What is one verse that stood out to you today?

Truth: What is one truth that you discovered about God or about life from today's reading?

Trust: What is one thing that you need to trust God with today?

Praise: What is one thing that you can praise God for today?

Week 1: Day Five

Read: Isaiah 1, Isaiah 8:11-9:7

Scripture: What is one verse that stood out to you today?

```
```

Truth: What is one truth that you discovered about God or about life from today's reading?

```
```

Trust: What is one thing that you need to trust God with today?

```
```

Praise: What is one thing that you can praise God for today?

```
```

Week 1 Review

Memorization: What is one or two verses that you want to memorize or write on your mind?

Application: How have you applied God's truth to your life this past week?

Praise: How has God helped or answered prayers this week?

Made in the USA
Columbia, SC
30 November 2022

72264526R00052